Bethlehem: The History and Lega of Jesus

By Charles River Editors

Daniel Case's picture of Bethlehem taken from the Church of the Nativity

About Charles River Editors

Charles River Editors is a boutique digital publishing company, specializing in bringing history back to life with educational and engaging books on a wide range of topics. Keep up to date with our new and free offerings with this 5 second sign up on our weekly mailing list, and visit Our Kindle Author Page to see other recently published Kindle titles.

We make these books for you and always want to know our readers' opinions, so we encourage you to leave reviews and look forward to publishing new and exciting titles each week.

Introduction

A 1698 sketch of Bethlehem

Bethlehem

"But as for you, Bethlehem Ephrathah,

Too little to be among the clans of Judah,

From you One will go forth for Me to be ruler in Israel

His goings forth are from long ago,

From the days of eternity." – The Book of Micah, Chapter 5

   Bethlehem is amongst the oldest cities in the world, one that has been conquered and ruled by Caananites, Jews, Romans, Arabs, Crusaders, the Mamluks of Egypt, and the Ottomans. In the last century alone, it has been controlled by various different parties. The British took Bethlehem during World War I and controlled the city from 1920-1948, and in the wake of the 1948 war between Israel and its neighbors, Jordan annexed Bethlehem and controlled it until the Six Day War in 1967. It was during the Six Day War that Israel took control of Bethlehem, remaining in power over the city until 1995, when, in compliance with the Oslo Peace Accords, control of the city and of the surrounding West Bank was handed over to the Palestinian National Authority. The Palestinians continue to administer affairs in Bethlehem to the present day. What was it that caused this one small, unassuming settlement to be the focus of so much attention and strife?

The primary reason that Bethlehem is so famous today is the Biblical passages that relate the town as the birthplace of Jesus Christ. Moreover, the oldest continuously used Christian church in the world is the Church of the Nativity in Bethlehem. Like the town itself, the Church of the Nativity has gone through numerous cycles of creation and ruin. First built above the Cave of the Nativity by Emperor Constantine's mother, Helena, in May 339, the church existed for almost two centuries before it was destroyed during the Samarian revolt in 529 CE. The church was later reconstructed by the Byzantine emperor Justinian in 565, and it is this structure that has largely survived to the present day. Today, the Church of the Nativity is a UNESCO World Heritage Site, alongside the pilgrimage route that led between Bethlehem and Jerusalem.

The church and its surrounding complex of convents, monasteries, and chapels are fortress-like in appearance, reflecting the turbulent history of not only Bethlehem but the religious communities connected to the site. It was a focal point in the conflicts of the Crusades, and like many other towns in the Holy Land it fell into decline after the European armies were forced from the Holy Land.

Despite being under Arab rule, Greek and Syrian Christian communities have continued to live and operate in the site, which was respected by both the Christian and Islamic faiths. It was also an important site for Judaism, being the location where many events of the Old Testament took place. Bethlehem is the burial place of Rachel, wife of Jacob, and it is where the story of Ruth and her mother-in-law Naomi took place. It was also known as the city of David because it was the place where King David was anointed by Samuel. Needless to say, all of its history and religious import make it one of the most important places on the planet.

Bethlehem: The History and Legacy of the Birthplace of Jesus looks at the history of the city and its importance in antiquity. Along with pictures depicting important people, places, and events, you will learn about Bethlehem like never before.

Ancient Origins

Bethlehem lies a little over 6 miles south of Jerusalem, standing at an elevation of over 2,000 feet above sea level. The town occupies a high position in the region, overlooking a landscape consisting of winding valleys, rocky hilltops, and a generally hot climate. This was the Kingdom of Judah, the Roman province of Judea, and one of the few agriculturally productive regions in the land known also as Ephrath (the "Fertile Land"). Bethlehem itself is situated east of the main road that leads between Jerusalem and Hebron, and the settlement is focused upon two limestone hills, one to the east and the other to the west. Most of the important ecclesiastical sites of Bethlehem are focused on the easternmost of these hills.[1]

Bethlehem is first mentioned in historical texts via the Amarna letters, dating from the 14th century BCE.[2] These were a series of letters sent to the Egyptian pharaohs by Canaanite and Assyrian kings, and in conjunction with that, one of the oldest traces of the ancient town of Bethlehem was recently discovered: a small clay bulla (seal) discovered in Jerusalem that was impressed with three brief lines in ancient Hebrew. The text has been interpreted as a tax record, evidence of a trade route that existed between Bethlehem and Jerusalem sometime in

---

[1] Ritter, C. (1968) *The comparative geography of Palestine and the Sinaitic Peninsula.* New York: Greenwood Press

[2] Ross, J. F. (1967) "Gezer in the Tell el-Amarna Letters." *The Biblical Archaeologist, 30*(2), 62 - 70.

the late 8th and 7th centuries BCE.[3]

More is known of the Roman settlement that developed at Bethlehem. In 63 BCE, the Roman general Pompey led his legions into the land of Judea. For more than a century Judea had been an independent nation, and many Jews believed that as the chosen people of the one true God they would remain free forever.[4] To the Jews, Judea was the Promised Land, given to them by God to be theirs alone, but it soon became clear that the world's strongest empire could not be resisted. What followed was one of the most chaotic and bloody periods in human history, with tensions and conflicts between Romans and Jews simmering in the 1st century BCE and the 1st century CE. The conflicts would culminate with wars that left Jerusalem and the Second Temple destroyed, but amid the chaos, two new religions began to flower, and they would change mankind's ideas about justice, mercy, and God.

[3] Antiquities Authority (2012) "Earliest Archaeological Evidence of the Existence of the City of Bethlehem already in the First Temple Period." Accessed: http://www.antiquities.org.il/Article_eng.aspx?sec_id=25&subj_id=240&id=1938&hist=1
[4] Goodman, M. (1993) *The ruling class of Judaea: the origins of the Jewish revolt against Rome, AD 66-70*. Cambridge: Cambridge University Press.

A bust of Pompey the Great

Jean Fouquet's painting *Pompey in the Temple of Jerusalem*

Bethlehem is first mentioned in the Bible as the burial site of Jacob's wife, Rachel: "Then they moved on from Bethel. While they were still some distance from Ephrath, Rachel began to give birth and had great difficulty... So Rachel died and was buried on the way to Ephrath (that is,

Bethlehem). Over her tomb Jacob set up a pillar, and to this day that pillar marks Rachel's tomb."[5] Rachel's tomb is located a short distance north of Bethlehem, on the road between Jerusalem and Hebron. It consists of a small building with a white dome erected during the Crusader period, though the original structure is obscured by modern defensive fortifications that have been erected around the site. The place has been an important site for Jewish, Christian, and Muslim pilgrims for millennia.[6]

RACHEL'S TOMB.
The terraced hills of Beit Jâla, the ancient Giloh, in the background.

A 19th century depiction of Rachel's Tomb

[5] Genesis, 35, 16 - 20
[6] Gonen, R. (2000) *Biblical Holy Places: an illustrated guide*. Paulist Press.

A 1930s picture of Rachel's Tomb

Bethlehem also figures prominently in the story of Ruth, a gentile who became the great-grandmother of David. She is said to have escaped from a famine in Bethlehem to Moab, a neighboring country, where she married a Jewish man named Chilion, who died shortly afterwards. She then traveled back to Bethlehem with her mother-in-law, Naomi. The town is described in this story as the "House of Bread" (in Arabic, the name means "House of Meat").[7] The two women arrived in time for the harvest, and Ruth started working in the barley fields surrounding Bethlehem. There she met a man named Boaz, who first helped her acquire land in the town and later had a child

---

[7] Ruth, 1, 19 - 22

with her.[8] This child, Obed, was the father of Jesse, the father of David who was born in Bethlehem and who would later become the second King of Israel.[9] David was anointed king by the prophet Samuel in Bethlehem.[10]

A 3ʳᵈ century CE depiction of Samuel anointing

---

[8] Ruth, 4, 1 - 12
[9] Ruth, 4, 13 - 22
[10] 1 Samuel, 16

David

One of the most important sites of Roman Bethlehem was the Herodium, a volcano-shaped mountain less than 4 miles southeast of Bethlehem upon which Herod the Great erected his fortress-palace. Herod the Great ruled over Judea between 37 and 4 BCE. He was victorious in battle against the last king of the Hasmonean dynasty, Antigonus, a battle that is believed to have taken place in the vicinity of Bethlehem.[11] Construction of his fortress began in 25 BCE,[12] and many thousands of slaves were brought to artificially shape the mountain and erect what would become the third largest palace in the Roman world. The building was seven stories high and protected by two massive concentric walls. The 1st century CE historian Josephus wrote of the Herodium: "This fortress… is naturally strong and very suitable for such a structure, for reasonably nearby is a hill, raised to a height by the hand of man and rounded off in the shape of a breast. At intervals it has round towers, and it has a steep ascent formed of two hundred steps of hewn stone. Within it are costly royal apartments made for security and for ornament at the same time. At the base of the hill there are pleasure grounds built in such a way as to be worth seeing, among other things because of the way in which

[11] Richardson, P. (1996) *Herod: King of the Jews and Friend of the Romans.* University of South Carolina Press.
[12] Jacobson, D. M. (1984) "The Design of the Fortress of Herodium." *Zeitschrift des Deutschen Palästina-Vereins*, 127 - 136.

water, which is lacking in that place, is brought in from a distance and at great expense. The surrounding plain was built up as a city second to none, with the hill serving as an acropolis for the other dwellings."[13]

An aerial photo of Herodium

[13] Flavius, J. (1995) "Wars of the Jews." In Whiston W. (trans.) *The Complete Works of Josephus.* Grand Rapids: Kregel Publications.

Excavations of Herod's Palace

A bust believed to be of Josephus

According to Josephus, there was a city that surrounded the base of the mountain, and Josephus's account is supported by archaeological evidence. It contained some particularly fine examples of Roman hydraulic engineering, with an enormous artificial pool – more than twice the size of a modern Olympic swimming pool – that was fed by an aqueduct that carried water over a distance of more than 3.5 miles.[14]

---

[14] Jacobson, 1984

Ellen Ya'aran's panorama of excavations around Herodium

The building projects aside, the clash of cultures between the Romans and the Jews led to a number of vicious and bloody conflicts. After Herod's death, the Herodium continued to be used as a Roman stronghold during the First Jewish Revolt between 66 and 73 CE. Between 132 and 135 CE, it was used by the Jews during the Second Jewish Revolt, also known as the Bar Kokhba Revolt, after it was taken by the insurgent leader Simon bar Kokhba. The fortress was later converted into a Christian monastery, and three churches were built in the lower town.[15]

In 2007, archaeologists claimed to have discovered King Herod's tomb on the northeastern slope of the mountain. After having excavated in the area for more than 35 years, the leading archaeologist Ehud Netzer of the Hebrew University of Jerusalem uncovered fragments of a

---

[15] Jacobson, 1984

sarcophagus made of pink limestone originating from Jerusalem, within a two story mausoleum.[16]

Deror Avi's picture of the Tomb of Herod

Bethlehem in the New Testament

The focal point of Christian faith in the religious landscape in Bethlehem is a cave, first officially recognized by the Church in the 4th century CE, which

[16] Netzer, E., Kalman, Y., Porath, R., and Chachy-Laureys, R. (2010) "Preliminary report on Herod's mausoleum and theatre with a royal box at Herodium." *Journal of Roman Archaeology, 23,* 84 - 108.

local people and religious institutions have long venerated as the birthplace of Jesus Christ. By the 3rd century, Origen of Alexandria referenced the cave as a place believed by locals to be the birthplace of Jesus: "In Bethlehem the cave is pointed out where He was born, and the manger in the cave where He was wrapped in swaddling clothes. And the rumor is in those places, and among foreigners of the Faith, that indeed Jesus was born in this cave who is worshipped and reverenced by the Christians."

In reality, the precise location of the birth of Jesus is unknown, but Bethlehem at the time of Christ was a very small town, meaning that even if Jesus was not born in the precise spot around which the Church of the Nativity complex later grew, then it was likely at least within a few hundred feet of the site. As a result of its importance, architectural development at this site began as far back as the Byzantine period between the 4th and 7th centuries.

The prophet Micah had stated more than 700 years earlier that Jesus would be born in Bethlehem: "But you, Bethlehem Ephrathah, though you are small among the clans of Judah, out of you will come for me one who will be ruler over Israel, whose origins are from of old, from ancient times."[17]

---

[17] Micah, 5, 2

The foremost account of the birth of Jesus is in the book of Luke. Caesar Augustus had decreed that a census be made of the entire Roman world, meaning everyone had to return to the city of his or her ancestors and be registered for the "privilege" of paying taxes. Due to this decree, Joseph and Mary were forced to go to Bethlehem, where Jesus was eventually born. This was a journey of approximately 75 miles, a distance that Mary – then heavily pregnant – would not have been able to walk. She likely rode on a donkey, and four days into the journey Mary went into labor. Desperate to find a room as they arrived late in the day in Bethlehem, they found the city crowded with people who had all come for the census, so there was no accommodation for Mary and Joseph anywhere. According to Luke, "So Joseph also went up from the town of Nazareth in Galilee to Judea, to Bethlehem the town of David, because he belonged to the house and line of David. He went there to register with Mary, who was pledged to be married to him and was expecting a child. While they were there, the time came for the baby to be born, and she gave birth to her firstborn, a son. She wrapped him in cloths and placed him in a manger, because there was no guest room available for them."[18]

---

[18] Luke, 2, 4 - 7

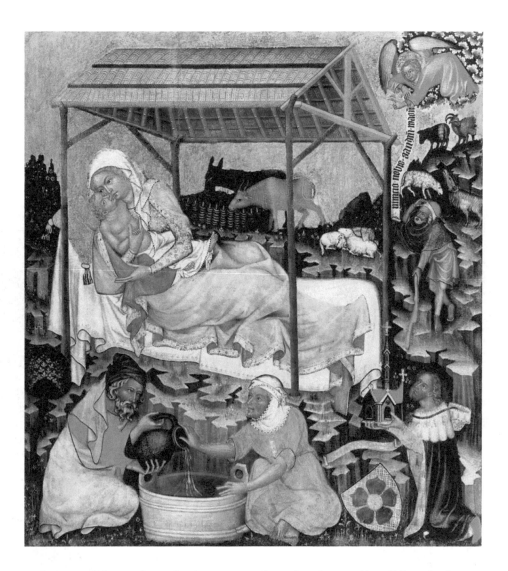

A medieval miniature depicting the Nativity

One of the key parts of the tale of the nativity was the announcement of Christ's birth to a group of shepherds that was made by an angel. Luke described this event: "And there were in the same country shepherds abiding in the field, keeping watch over their flock by night. And, lo, the angel of the Lord came upon them, and the glory of the Lord shone round about them: and they were sore afraid. And the angel said unto them, Fear not: for, behold, I bring you good tidings of great joy, which shall be to all people. For unto you is born this day in the city of David a Savior, which is Christ the Lord. And this shall be a sign unto you; ye shall find the babe wrapped in swaddling clothes, lying in a manger."[19]

***Adoration of the Shepherds* by Gerard van Honthorst**

There are three locations in the vicinity of Bethlehem that have been claimed to be the location where these events took place. The old town of Beit Sahour, located a

[19] Luke, 2, 8 - 12

short distance east of Bethlehem, is said to be the location where an angel announced to the shepherds that Jesus had been born. In the eastern part of the town is a convent established by Saint Helena, and later in 1347 it was acquired by the Order of Saint Francis.[20] This red rock, domed church is also identified as the Tower of Edar, where Jacob resided following the death of his wife, Rachel.[21] This place is linked to the shepherd's story by Eusebius, a bishop of Caesarea in the 4th century.[22] Pilgrims can still visit the old grottoes in which shepherds used to live during the time of Christ.[23] The subterranean caves contain mosaics and frescoes, as well as a Latin altar, which would have been created by the community of Saint Helena's convent.[24]

---

[20] de Cree, F. (1999) "History and Archaeology of the Bēt Sāḥūr Region. A Preparatory Study for a Regional Survey (The Bethlehem Archaeological Project)." *Zeitschrift des Deutschen Palästina-Vereins*, 59 - 84.

[21] Hutchinson, R. F. (1887) "The Tower of Edar." *Palestine Exploration Quarterly*, *19*(3), 167 - 169.

[22] de Cree, 1999

[23] The site also has significance for the Arab people, as it contains a shrine to Sheikh Ahmad al-Sahuri, an 18th century saint. See Sharon, M. (2009). *Corpus Inscriptionum Arabicarum Palaestinae,(CIAP). Volume Two, B – C. Handbook of Oriental studies: The Near and Middle East 30*. Brill Academic Publishers

[24] Conder, C. R. (1881) *The Survey of Western Palestine*. Committee of the Palestine Exploration Fund

The Church at Shepherds' Field

The second potential site where the shepherd's tale took place is north of Beit Sahour. Roughly 1200 feet north of Saint Helena's convent can be found a tent-shaped Greek chapel called the Chapel of the Angels, which is built upon and incorporates elements of an early 4th century church and later monastery. Ancient frescoes within the church depict the shepherds receiving the good news from the angel, and their journey to Bethlehem to pay homage to the newborn child.[25] The roof was designed by the Italian architect Antonio Barluzzi, and it features

[25] Baedeker, K. (1876) *Palestine and Syria, handbook for travelers*. Leipzig: Karl Baedeker Publisher.

hundreds of small circular skylights. A small grotto is also found in the vicinity of the church.[26]

The third location is to the east of Beit Sahour, where an additional cave system has been discovered with the remains of ancient ceramics.[27]

The final major actors in the story of the birth of Jesus are the three wise men of the east, though it is unlikely that the Magi were actually present on the night that Jesus was born.

Luke indicates that Joseph and Mary brought Jesus to the Temple in Jerusalem 40 days after Jesus was born, which means they had remained in Bethlehem for some time after his birth: "And when the days for their purification according to the law of Moses were completed, they brought Him up to Jerusalem to present Him to the Lord."[28] In fact, in the course of describing the visit of the Magi, the Bible clearly notes there had been time enough for Joseph and Mary to find a house in Bethlehem: "On coming to the house, they saw the child with his mother Mary, and they bowed down and worshiped him. Then they opened their treasures and presented him with gifts of gold, frankincense and myrrh. And having been warned in

---

[26] Baedeker, 1876

[27] This site is also known as the Field of Boaz, and is connected to the Old Testament figure of Ruth, the great-grandmother of King David. See Young, P. (1999) "Bethlehem's second big day." *History Today*, 49(11), 6.

[28] Luke, 2, 22

a dream not to go back to Herod, they returned to their country by another route."[29]

These Magi were wealthy and well-educated. They likely came from Persia, but they had been ordered by King Herod to discover the location of Christ, purportedly so that Herod could pay homage to the child, but in all likelihood to murder the newborn threat to his power. Word quickly reached King Herod of the arrival of a newborn "King of the Jews," and as he was understandably unwilling to allow any threat to his own authority, Herod was determined to do away with this child. He sent soldiers to kill all of the boys that were up to two years old in and around Bethlehem – an event known as the "Massacre of the Innocents".[30] It was a tragic event for many families in the city, but Jesus was evidently safe on his way to Egypt with his parents.

---

[29] Matthew, 2, 11 - 12
[30] France, R. T. (1979) "Herod and the Children of Bethlehem." *Novum Testamentum*, *21*(2), 98 - 120.

A Byzantine mosaic depicting the Magi

The Adoration of the Magi by Bartolomé Esteban
Murillo

The Church of the Nativity

According to some scholars, the Cave of the Nativity was originally a shrine dedicated to Adonis, also known as Tammuz.[31] Adonis-Tammuz was a god of vegetation, youth, and the cycle of life and death who was worshiped across the lands of Sumer and Mesopotamia, and the god was later integrated into the Greek pantheon.

The renowned Dalmatian theologian and confessor, Saint Jerome, visited Bethlehem on a number of occasions during his lifetime as part of the regular pilgrimages that he made between Jerusalem and other holy sites in the land.[32] In 388 he returned to Bethlehem, and he spent the rest of his life residing and working within this cave.[33] After 35 years of work translating the Scriptures from Hebrew and Greek into Latin in the subterranean study, he produced his seminal work of writing, the "*Vulgate*".[34] In his writings, Jerome reported that the cave had been originally consecrated by heathen Adonis worshippers, and that they cultivated a sacred grove at the mouth of the cave.[35] Saint Jerome is said to have died in the cave in September 420 and was originally buried there, but his

---

[31] Rapp, D. (2015) *The Church of the Nativity in Bethlehem*. Hanan Isachar.

[32] Coxe, A. C. (1998) *Jerome: his life, writings, and controversies*. Hendrickson Pub.

[33] Coxe, 1998

[34] The *Vulgate* was the Latin version of the Bible which remained the authoritative edition used by the Catholic Church until the 20th century, a version that was "assuredly heard by more Christians than any other" (Freeman-Grenville, G. S. P. (1996) *The Holy Land: A Pilgrim's Guide to Israel, Jordan, and the Sinai*. Continuum)

[35] Taylor, J. E. (1993) *Christians and the holy places: The myth of Jewish-Christian origins*. Oxford: Oxford University Press.

remains were later brought Constantinople and then to Rome, where they are currently kept in the Basilica of St Mary Major.[36]

Artin Afsharjavan's picture of a statue of Saint Jerome in Bethlehem

[36] Coxe, 1998

There are a lot more caves in Bethlehem than just the Cave of the Nativity. In fact, a vast cave network exists beneath the town, and they have been excavated, modified, and used for various purposes throughout the ages.[37] There were the study and tomb of Saint Jerome, as well as the spot of the Tomb of Eusebius, who succeeded Jerome and served as bishop of Caesarea. There were also the tombs of St Paula and her daughter Eustochium, the female companions of Jerome who followed him on his pilgrimage in 485 and eventually settled in Bethlehem. The cave network also holds the subterranean Chapel of Saint Joseph, dedicated to the husband of the Virgin Mary, and the Chapel of the Innocents, which holds the buried remains of the victims of the massacre ordered by Herod the Great when he heard of the birth of Christ.

The original basilican Church of the Nativity was built between 326 and 339 under the patronage of Emperor Constantine I and Empress Helena of Rome.[38] Parts of this early structure, including its foundations, have survived underground to the present day and have provided researchers with a sense of what the original structure looked like. The sacred grove of the Adonis-Tammuz was cleared away, and the cave itself was worked on to modify the space to serve the requirements of Christian rituals and

---

[37] Prag, K. (2000) "Bethlehem: a site assessment." *Palestine exploration quarterly*, *132*(2), 169 - 181.
[38] Freeman-Grenville, G. S. P. (1993) *The basilica of the nativity in Bethlehem*. Carta the Israel Map and Publishing Company Limited.

ceremonies. The natural rock ceiling of the cave was pierced, leading through a shaft to a circular opening above. This was then surrounded by a raised octagonal stone balustrade, itself surrounded by an *ambulatorium* – a walkway that pilgrims would follow.[39] These worshippers would be able to access the *ambulatorium* by two staircases, one for ascending and the other for descending, to view the interior of the cave without actually entering the sacred space. The cave, balustrade, and walkway were enclosed within an octagonal shaped structure. On its roof and directly above the cave was a round oculus through which sunlight would fill the space within.[40] This was the core of a basilican church that extended to the west. It consisted of five aisles divided by four rows of columns, decorated with capitals in the Corinthian order. They led to an atrium with an open roof and colonnaded portico, with the main entrance to the complex to the west.[41] The entire structure was a little over 70 feet long, and contemporary writers mentioned the riches that the church contained, including gold and silver objects studded with precious jewels, beautifully embroidered fabrics, marble sculptures, and frescoes. The floors and walls were decorated with mosaics. The center of attention was a silver manger, replacing an original clay one.[42]

---

[39] Freeman-Grenville, 1993
[40] Freeman-Grenville, 1993
[41] Freeman-Grenville, 1993

Jean-Christophe Benoist's picture of a bust of Constantine

In 529, as a result of the Samaritan Revolts between the Samaritans and Byzantine Empire, Constantine's Church was destroyed by fire. A deep layer of ash, scorched wood, and broken building material has since been

---

[42] Freeman-Grenville, 1993

discovered by archaeologists above a layer of mosaics from the Constantinian church.

The 4th century church was later replaced by the building that exists in present-day Bethlehem. Between 530 and 533, Emperor Justinian I dedicated a second Church of the Nativity upon the site, and according to the Egyptian Patriarch Eutychius of Alexandria, the Church of the Nativity in Bethlehem was destroyed and rebuilt by Justinian because the Byzantine emperor felt that the old church was too small.[43] This is the oldest Christian church that has remained in constant use throughout history.

---

[43] Freeman-Grenville, 1993

A contemporary mosaic of Justinian the Great

The new church was very different from that which existed before. The size and form of the nave were roughly the same as the previous church, but a narthex was added to the western end of the church, making the old atrium smaller and adding three monumental doorways on its eastern side. The *ambulatorium* and octagonal structure above the cave were removed and replaced by a much larger space, an extension of the nave with apses to the north, east, and south. A chancel and altar could then be installed in the church, allowing large religious services to be held within the space.[44] The new structure was covered with a massive vaulted roof, later supported by wooden scaffolding that has survived to the present day.

[44] Hamilton, R. W. (1968) *The Church of the Nativity, Bethlehem: A Guide*. Department of Antiquities and Museums, Ministry of Education and Culture.

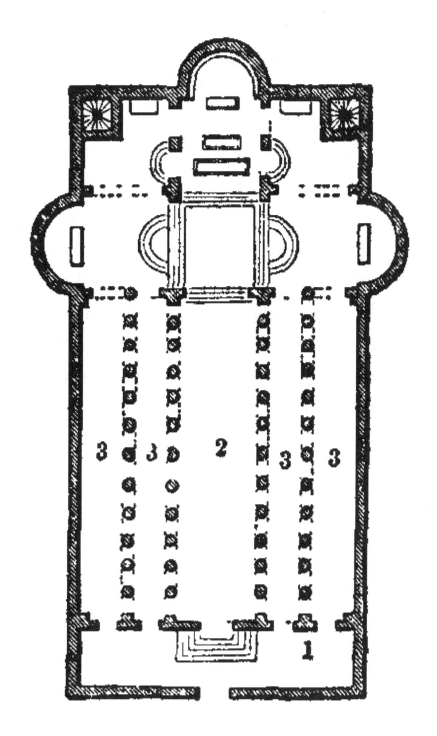

An early 20ᵗʰ century blueprint with the layout of the church

The layout of the church was still specifically tailored for the needs of pilgrims visiting Bethlehem; they could enter the church via the atrium, congregate within the narthex, and then proceed through the church proper along the aide aisle. An octagonal baptismal font made of local red limestone was positioned in the southern aisle, dating from sometime between the 6th and 7th centuries. It would have been used by those newly converting to the Christian faith, who would only be allowed to access the church after their baptism.[45] Reaching the chancel area, they could then descend via one staircase to the Cave of the Nativity before ascending from the other staircase and leaving the church along the opposite side aisle. This meant that both pilgrims and worshippers attending a religious service could make use of the church at the same time.

The columns in the nave of Justinian's church contained 46 columns that shared the Corinthian capitals used in Constantine's church, though these were newly made and not reused from the previous church. They were made of locally quarried red limestone and polished to the point that they resembled marble.[46] The capitals supported a horizontal line of timber "tie beams" connecting the rafters of the roof, coated in plaster and elaborately decorated. Traces of the paintings that originally decorated the church interior have been preserved in these

---

[45] Beginning in the 12th century new stories began to be associated with the font. One was that this was where the star fell after it had guided the three wise men to Bethlehem. Another was that this tapped into a water source that was used by David. See Hamilton, 1968
[46] Freeman-Grenville, 1993

isolated areas of the building, most of them dating to the Crusader period. This makes the paintings of the Church of the Nativity one of the best surviving corpuses of art from the Latin Kingdom of Jerusalem dating from the 12th century.

These paintings depicted Christian male and female saints that had lived in Palestine, icons, bishops, deacons, laity, kings, monks, nuns, scenes in the life of Jesus Christ, and depictions of the Virgin Mary with child. Some of the saints were commemorated for both the Eastern and Western Christian orders, such as St Sabas, St Theodosius, and St Euthym. Amongst the figures in the church illustrations were Olaf, king of Norway, and Canute, king of Denmark and England.[47] A masterpiece amid the paintings is that of John the Baptist, with a highly developed three dimensional style and exquisitely detailed clothing. It is unlikely that a single painter created all of these pictures; instead, it seems there was a school of religious art that flourished in Bethlehem around the 12th century.

One of the oldest paintings in the church is of the Virgin Mary Enthroned, an icon dating from the late 16h century. It is believed to have been brought to Bethlehem from the Holy Lavra of Saint Sabbas the Sanctified, a Greek Orthodox monastery in the Judean Desert halfway

---

[47] Freeman-Grenville, 1993

between Jerusalem and the Dead Sea.[48] Other icons in the church are attributed to the Arab Melkites, a Catholic denomination in the Middle East who followed Byzantine rites.[49]

Ian and Wendy Sewell's picture of an icon of the

[48] Hamilton, 1968
[49] Hamilton, 1968

Virgin Mary and Jesus

The altar

Some of the pictures in the church are believed to have been produced by a 17th century painter named Jeremiah Paladas. Originally from Crete, he became a monk at St Catherine's Monastery on Mount Sinai between 1602 and 1639 before painting in Bethlehem. His work can also be found in the Church of the Holy Sepulchre in Jerusalem, the church in St Catherine's Monastery in Sinai, and the cathedral in the Old Patriarchate in Cairo.[50]

---

[50] Evseeva, L. M. (2005) *A History of Icon Painting: Sources, Traditions, Present Day*. Grand Holding Publishers.

Another Cretan artist, Victor the Cretan (ca. 1651 – 1697), worked in Bethlehem and left behind particularly fine images on the iconostasis of the nearby Chapel of Saint George.[51] These include an Eleusa icon (the Virgin Mary with Christ held close to her cheek), and another of Christ painted upon a partly burnt cross that has been dated to 1681.[52]

The majority of the icons can be found on the wooden iconostasis – wall of icons – positioned in front of the eastern apse inside the basilica. Much of the iconostasis was damaged in the fire of 1869, but the icons have been restored or reconstructed anew.[53] It consists of three rows of paintings. The bottom row frames the entrance to the sanctuary. To the right of the gateway is the figure of Christ Pantocrator, a specific manner of depicting Christ "almighty" or "omnipotent". To the left is an icon of Theotokos, Mary the "Mother of God", alongside a number of saints. Above this is a row that depicts the 12 main feasts of the year in the Eastern Orthodox Church (see table). The topmost tier depicts the Deesis, a representation of the Virgin Mary, Saint John the Baptist, and Christ Pantocrator. The iconostasis is topped with a text that reads, "Presented from his Excellency the Metropolis of Kyrenia Dio Necios to the Holy Land

---

[51] Evseeva, 2005
[52] Prag, 2000
[53] Hamilton, 1968

1853".[54] Kyrenia was a city in northern Cyprus, under Ottoman rule at the time of the construction of this iconostasis.

Feast	Date
The Nativity of the Theotokos	September 8th
The Exaltation of the Cross	September 14th
The Presentation of the Theotokos	November 21st
The Nativity of Christ/Christmas	December 25th
The Baptism of Christ (Theophany / Epiphany)	January 6th
The Presentation of Jesus at the Temple	February 2nd
The Annunciation	March 25th
The Entry into Jerusalem or Flowery/Willow/Palm Sunday	Sunday before Pascha (Easter)
The Ascension of Christ	40 days after Pascha
Pentecost	50 days after Pascha

54 Hamilton, 1968

The Transfiguration	August 6th
The Dormition (Falling Asleep) of the Theotokos	August 15th

Of equal, if not greater, magnificence was the mosaic art that once decorated the walls and floor of the church nave. Remains of these mosaics have been discovered on two walls dating from the Crusader period. That of the south wall depicts the seven General Ecumenical Councils of the Church: the First Council of Nicaea, the First Council of Constantinople, the Councils of Ephesus and Chalcedon, the Second Council of Constantinople, the Third Council of Constantinople, and the Second Council of Nicaea.[55] The mosaic of the north wall depicted the Six Provincial Councils of the Greeks – Ancyra, Antioch, Sardica, Gangrae, Laodicea, and Carthage – of which only Antioch and Sardica survive in the present day.[56] One thing that these two scenes share is the theme of administration, indicating the central role of following dogma that both the Western and Eastern churches shared.

Less is known of the mosaics that covered the western and eastern walls of the nave, though documentary records from the 18th century onwards has given a partial description. To the west was an image of the Tree of

---

[55] Hunt, L. A. (1991) "Art and Colonialism: The Mosaics of the Church of the Nativity in Bethlehem (1169) and the Problem of" Crusader" Art." *Dumbarton Oaks Papers*, *45*, 69 - 85.
[56] Hunt, 1991

Jesse, showing the ancestors of Jesus Christ alongside other figures, including prophets.[57] These include Sibyl, a prophetess and priest of Apollo at Cumae (a Greek colony near present-day Naples) who became venerated during the Middle Ages as one of those that prophesized the birth of Christ.[58] The donkey of Balaam was also depicted on one of the walls.[59] On the eastern side of the nave were images from the New Testament, but most of their details have been lost to time. These depicted scenes from the life of Jesus, including the Annunciation, the Nativity, the entrance of Jesus into Jerusalem, and the Last Supper.[60] A mosaic decorated the semi-spherical alcove above the church altar, though this was heavily damaged in 1873.[61] It might have been this mosaic that depicted the three Magi at the Nativity – the image that is attributed to the church's survival during the Persian invasion of 614.[62]

Mosaics were also found on the church floor. Around 80 centimeters below the present-day tiled red stone slabs has been found a layer of magnificent mosaic designs dating from the time of Constantine. The patterns were geometric with vegetal elements, and within one of the designs is the Greek word "fish", which had much relevance to the

[57] Hunt, 1991

[58] Pelikan, J. (1978) *The Christian Tradition: A History of the Development of Doctrine, Volume 3: The Growth of Medieval Theology (600-1300)*. University of Chicago Press.

[59] See Numbers, 22, 21 - 39

[60] Hunt, 1991

[61] Hunt, 1991

[62] Harvey, W., Lethaby, W. R., Dalton, O. M., Cruso, H. A. A., Headlam, A. C., and Schultz, R. W. (1911) *The Church of the Nativity at Bethlehem*. London: B. T. Batsford

narrative of Christ. The "Chi-Ro" inscription is also found on the mosaics.[63]

Ian and Wendy Sewell's picture of the 4th century mosaic unearthed in the church

Marvelous as the Church of the Nativity was, the focal

[63] Kitzinger, E. (1970) *The Threshold of the Holy Shrine: Observations on the Floor Mosaics at Antioch and Bethlehem*.

point for any visitor to the complex was the cave underneath it, the cave where Jesus is believed to have been born. The cave was accessed by two flights of stairs that lead into a semi-conical space, where the door to the grotto could be found. The door itself is notable; it is covered with red and silver curtains, and the bronze door leaves date from the Crusader period.[64] Through the door, another flight of stairs leads even further beneath the church. The Cave of the Nativity had walls lined with marble and covered with silks and painted linen, and floors of marble slabs. It contains a Byzantine mosaic depicting the nativity, and one of the Virgin Mary with unique Latin inscriptions.[65] There is a hole in the northwestern corner of the cave said to be the location where the Star of Bethlehem fell after the three Magi had been guided to the birthplace of Christ.[66]

On the opposite corner of the space is a doorway that leads to a second cave, located north of the Church of the Nativity close to the Church of Saint Catherine. Still further caves lead off from these subterranean passages, and the complete plan of the underground complex remains unknown to this day.

---

[64] Freeman-Grenville, 1993
[65] Hunt, 1991
[66] Freeman-Grenville, 1993

A medieval depiction of the church

A 19ᵗʰ century depiction of the interior

20ᵗʰ century pictures of the interior

A modern picture of the interior

Bethlehem in the Holy Land

From approximately 386 and on, a number of convents were developed in the vicinity of the Church of the Nativity for both men and women. The two earliest convents were devoted to Saint Jerome and his female companions, Paula and Eustochium.[67] Together, these three figures strove to make Bethlehem one of the primary monastic centers of the Holy Land, a status that continued to develop into the Crusader period and beyond.

Between the 3rd and 7th centuries, a series of conflicts broke out between the Eastern Roman Empire and the Sasanian dynasty of the Persian Empire. During the Byzantine-Sasanian War of 602-628 the Sasanians captured Jerusalem, and went on to conquer much of Judea. When the Persians invaded Palestine in the seventh century they destroyed many of the Christian churches that they came upon. However, they left the Church of the Nativity intact. Legend has it that they were moved by a nativity painting within the church that depicted the wise men from the east in Persian clothing.[68]

Around the year 622, the early Muslim conquests of the Rashidun and Umayyad caliphates began to bring about about the collapse of the Sasanian Empire. Islam spread throughout the conquered territories. During the early

---

[67] Pringle, D. (1993) *The Churches of the Crusader Kingdom of Jerusalem*. Cambridge University Press.
[68] Hamilton, 1968

Islamic period between the 7th and 11th centuries, Bethlehem came under the dominion of the Muslim caliphates, and in 634, Modestus, the Patriarch of Jerusalem, failed to celebrate Christmas in Bethlehem for the first time in three centuries.[69]

During this time, parts of the southern transept of Justinian's church were converted to be used as prayer areas for Muslims.[70] Bethlehem was an important site for Muslims, who considered it the birthplace of Issa, the Islamic equivalent of Jesus who was seen as a prophet for the coming of Muhammad. In 1009, Caliph Hakim ordered that Christian monuments and structures around the Holy Land be destroyed, but the Church of the Nativity managed to survive this widespread destruction.[71]

Whereas under the Fatimids relative peace existed between the Muslims and pilgrims from other faiths that traveled to Jerusalem and other sites in the Holy Land, a new threat emerged during the 11th century with the growth in power of the Rum Seljuks in Anatolia. These Turkish tribes expanded west and south across Syria and Palestine, and in 1076 they conquered Jerusalem, pillaging the holy city and slaughtering its residents.[72]

---

[69] Pringle, 1993
[70] Pringle, 1993
[71] Pringle, 1993
[72] Cahen, C. (1988) *The Seljukid Sultanate of Rum, Eleventh to Fourteenth Centuries.* London: Longman

In response, Pope Urban II called for the First Crusade to liberate the Holy Land at the Council of Clermont in 1095, sparking a series of invasions from Europe that would transform the Near East. It was during the 12th century that Bethlehem once again became a place for the coronation of kings, and during the First Crusade the major states and kingdoms of the Holy Land were established, first at Edessa and then Antioch.[73] The Crusaders reclaimed Jerusalem in July 1099, and on Christmas Day in 1100, Baldwin I was crowned as king of the Latin Kingdom of Jerusalem in the Church of the Nativity. His successor, Baldwin II, was also crowned there in 1119.[74]

[73] Venning, T. (2015) *A Chronology of the Crusades*. London: Routledge
[74] Venning, 2015

A depiction of Pope Urban II calling for the First Crusade

A medieval depiction of King Baldwin I of Jerusalem

Bethlehem was occupied by the Crusaders between 1099 and 1187, and a hospital and a hospice for pilgrims were constructed in the town during this time. The Church of the Nativity was heavily modified, with the construction of two bell towers on either side of the church narthex. The grand doorways of the narthex were bricked up and replaced by a single much smaller iron door. In 1130, the church acquired the body of Joseph of Arimathea, the man who moved Jesus from his cross into the tomb of his burial and rebirth. His body was positioned to the west of the church choir, close to the chancel screen.[75] At the same time, a series of paintings were positioned around the church, as well as icons depicting the Virgin and Child.[76]

---

[75] Hamilton, 1968

Between 1160 and 1169, parts of the church were restored, and the context of these restorations was very significant in terms of the relationship between the Western and Eastern churches. At some point between 1167 and 1169, the King of Jerusalem, Amalric, negotiated an alliance with the Emperor of Byzantium, Manuel I Komnenos. They agreed that Amalric would marry the daughter of Manuel, Princess Maria. Amalric was later succeeded by his son, King Baldwin IV of Jerusalem, who continued to foster close relations between Byzantium and the Crusader state forged by his father.[77] The most important outcome from these events was a debate between the Orthodox, Catholic, and Eastern Christian churches, which all agreed to collaborate on a restoration of the Church of the Nativity in Bethlehem.

As a result, around the year 1165, the main altar and the crypt were rebuilt by the Crusaders. The wall mosaics were refurbished by a monk named Ephraim, who added to the church mosaics a number of trilingual texts that reflect the cosmopolitan nature of Bethlehem during this time.[78] Latin, Greek, and Syriac were all used to represent the Catholic, Orthodox, and the Monophysite communities that began to occupy Bethlehem from the 1160s.[79]

[76] Hamilton, 1968
[77] Jones, L., and Maguire, H. (2002) "A description of the jousts of Manuel I Komnenos." *Byzantine and Modern Greek Studies*, *26*(1), 104 - 148.
[78] Hunt, 1991

From the standpoint of the Europeans and Byzantines, the First Crusade was a great success, and it shaped the politics, religious affairs, and economy throughout the rest of the Middle Ages. However, more conflict was to come. In 1169, Saladin conquered Egypt and established the Ayyubid dynasty soon after. He then embarked on a number of campaigns to expand his territory northwards into the Levant, and he specifically focused his attention on reclaiming the lost Arab territories in Palestine and Syria. Although the Europeans were quick to respond by launching a Second Crusade in the 1140s, they suffered a crippling defeat at the Battle of Marj Ayyun in 1179. Saladin captured Bethlehem in September 1187.[80]

The Crusaders managed to recapture Bethlehem in the early 1190s, and in 1227 two wooden doors were installed at the threshold between the narthex and nave of the church. These were gifts sent by Constantine, King of Armenia, and were inscribed in Arabic and Armenian surrounded by carved flowers and crosses. The Armenian text read, "The door of the Blessed Mother of God was made in the year 676 by the hands of the Father Abraham and Father Arakel in the time of Hethum son of Constantine, King of Armenia. God have mercy on their souls."[81] The Arabic inscription read, "This door was

[79] Hunt, L. A. (1991) "Art and Colonialism: The Mosaics of the Church of the Nativity in Bethlehem (1169) and the Problem of" Crusader" Art." *Dumbarton Oaks Papers*, *45*, 69 - 85.

[80] Venning, 2015

[81] Hamilton, 1968

finished with the help of God (be He exalted), in the days of our Lord the Sultan Malik al–Mu'azzam in the month of Muharram in the year 624 H."[82]

Bethlehem came under the control of the Franks in 1229, but there is evidence that during the 1240s much damage was caused to the church, and many of its possessions went missing or were destroyed.[83] In April 1244, Bethlehem was taken over by the Khwarezmians Turks, and in 1263, the monastery at Bethlehem was destroyed by the Mamluk sultan, Baybers. Three years later, the Latin residents of the town were expelled, but from May 1271 Latin pilgrims were once again allowed to travel to Bethlehem.[84]

In 1277, the Eastern Orthodox Church congregation of the Western Rite Orthodoxy was again allowed into the Church of the Nativity, and from this point onwards, the stewardship of the Church of the Nativity came under the Greek Orthodox Church.[85] Under their guardianship, the church building was modified between the 12th and 13th centuries. The side doors of the narthex were closed and bricked up, while the main door on the western side of the building was reduced in size. The entrance to the church was made this small so as to prevent marauders from

---

[82] Hamilton, 1968
[83] Prag, 2000
[84] Freeman-Grenville, 1993
[85] Freeman-Grenville, 1993

entering the basilica on horseback. It is now referred to as the "Door of Humility" because each visitor must bow down to enter.[86]

Ian and Wendy Sewell's picture of the Door of Humility, the main entrance to the church

[86] Freeman-Grenville, 1993

Further repairs to the church were made in 1448. Philip, the Duke of Burgundy, had successfully petitioned to Pope Nicolas V to send artisans and materials from Jerusalem to Bethlehem to repair the roof of the Church of the Nativity,[87] but for unknown reasons the work was not carried out, and by 1461 the roof timbers in the church were rotting. Each day the building was falling further into ruin, until two decades later, in 1480, King Edward IV of England donated funds to send wood from Venice to Bethlehem to restore the roof. These repairs were carried out by a man named Tomacello, the Guardian of Mount Zion.[88]

Since the 11th century, the Church of the Nativity has found itself part of a much larger and more complex religious landscape. A number of ecclesiastical buildings – shrines, chapels, monasteries and convents – have been constructed over the centuries in the area surrounding the sacred cave, and they have become an inextricable part of Bethlehem's story and present-day heritage significance.

One of these is the Church of Saint Catherine of Alexandria, commonly known as Saint Catherine's. It is located immediately north of the Church of the Nativity, and was directly accessible from the basilica via a door in the western wall that leads into a colonnaded courtyard of

[87] Hamilton, 1968
[88] Harvey, Lethaby, Dalton, Cruso, Headlam, and Schultz, 1911

Saint Augustine's, a 12th century Crusader monastery. Saint Catherine's was constructed in the 15th century, and served as the main center of the Roman Catholic community in Bethlehem ever since.[89] The structure was in the form of an extended 80 x 20 foot basilica consisting of a nave and choir. A small chapter house dating from the original convent of Saint Augustine was incorporated into the structure.[90] Dormitories were built on the northern side of the church. A locked door within the church leads to the subterranean caves underneath the town.[91] The church also features five bells made in 1882 inscribed with Latin phrases and images of the Virgin Mary and a number of saints.[92]

Between 1874 and 1882, and again in 1949, the Church of Saint Catherine expanded, integrating elements of the Church of the Nativity, Franciscan Monastery, and Saint Helena's Chapel into its plan. The Catholics celebrate mass on December 25th, and on this occasion a statue of the child of Christ is brought from the Church of Saint Catherine to be placed in the grotto beneath the Church of the Nativity. The statue stays there until January 6th – the date of Epiphany – when it is returned to the Church of Saint Catherine.[93]

---

[89] Prag, 2000
[90] Pringle, 1993
[91] Prag, 2000
[92] Prag, 2000
[93] Raheb, M., Strickert, F., Strickert, F. M., and Nalbandian, G. (1998) *Bethlehem 2000: Past and Present*. Interlink Pub Group Inc.

Liad Malone's picture of the Church of St. Catherine of Alexandria

The northernmost of the bell towers added to the Church of the Nativity is Saint Helena's Chapel, owned and operated today by the Order of Saint Francis. Traces of Byzantine frescoes can still be seen on the east and west walls, and its vaulted ceiling still has much of the original plaster and whitewash that was applied centuries ago.[94] The southern half of the narthex is part of the Armenian Convent, which enjoys its own separate entrance to the church from the south. Unusually, even the vestibule of the narthex is divided between the different orders present

---

[94] Boas, A. J. (2005) *Crusader archaeology: the material culture of the Latin East.* London: Routledge.

in Bethlehem; most of it is owned by the Greek Orthodox Church, apart from two steps that are owned and maintained by the Armenian Church.[95]

The Order of Saint Francis was centered on the Franciscan Monastery, located north of the Church of Saint Catherine's. According to documentary records, the monastery was first built in the 12th century during the Crusader period.[96] It was first occupied by the Canons Regular of Saint Augustine, one of the oldest Western Church orders in history. It is believed by some that the monastery was built above the site of a convent founded by Saint Paula, the female companion of Saint Jerome during his pilgrimages.[97] The Franciscans have occupied the monastery since 1347.[98] The complex consisted of a central courtyard, around which were arranged a number of ecclesiastical buildings. Access to the Church of Saint Catherine's was through a door in the southern portico. A staircase nearby led to the underground cave system.[99] On the opposite side of the courtyard was the refectory; an unusual structure built on three barrel-vaulted levels due to the steep topography of the landscape.[100] Most of the eastern portion of the complex was destroyed when the

[95] Palestine Ministry of Tourism and Antiquities (2011) *Birthplace of Jesus: Church of the nativity and the pilgrimage route, a world heritage site nomination document.* UNESCO
[96] Boas, 2005
[97] Prag, 2000
[98] Pringle, 1993
[99] Prag, 2000
[100] Prag, 2000

Church of Saint Catherine was enlarged during the late 19th century.

To the south of the Church of the Nativity was the Armenian convent. Most of the complex was built in the 12th century, though there is some evidence of earlier structures adjacent to the basilica, and there were additions made in the 17th century and a bell tower constructed in 1930.[101] A staircase that led to the monks' dormitories was on the eastern side of the complex, as well as a doorway that led to the ecclesiastical gardens. There was a refectory, known later as the "School of Saint Jerome", which consisted of a splendid vaulted hall with the original columns and clerestory windows that fill the space with light.[102]

To the south and east of the Church of the Nativity was the Greek Orthodox Convent. Also built during the 12th century, the convent consists of a central rectangular building that is operated today as the Chapel of Saint George.[103] This is represented by a bas relief marble panel set into the western wall of the building. It depicts Saint George slaying the dragon.

A formidable tower was constructed on the southern side of the complex next to the sacristy, dating from as early as

[101] Prag, 2000
[102] Prag, 2000
[103] Prag, 2000

the 6th century. This may have served as a place of refuge for the community of Orthodox priests, or perhaps as a place to securely store their expensive artifacts and icons.

Also accessible via the Greek Orthodox Convent was a cave system used as a place of burial, found to the south of the Church of the Nativity and extending beneath its southern aisles and nave. The style of these chambers indicates that they were originally used during the Roman or Byzantine period.[104] It was also later associated with the massacre of the Holy Innocents by Herod the Great.

To the east of the Church of the Nativity was a plot of land that was owned in part by each of these different religious communities for gardens and pasture. These developed upon wide artificial terraces made of yellow limestone ashlar and rubble, some of them quite monumental at up to 7 meters high.[105] According to the records left behind by visitors to the town in the 18th and 19th centuries, massive stone walls one surrounded each of the small garden plots that were cultivated there, though today only a few dressed stone walls flank the gardens east of the Franciscan convent. In 1926, the Order of Saint Francis were clearing their area of the old own when they discovered 13 bells buried in the gardens sometime during the 14th century, perhaps under the orders of

---

[104] Prag, 2000
[105] Prag, 2000

Mohammed II in 1452.[106] The Armenian Orthodox Monastery also had their own gardens which, unlike the others, contain evidence of burials dating from the Iron Age II period.[107] When the White Sisters took over the responsibilities of this land in 1909, they discovered ceramics from the Iron Age II and Byzantine periods, which reinforces the theory that this was the location of a much earlier settlement.[108]

For most of the roughly 1,500 years that the Church of the Nativity has existed, Bethlehem and its ecclesiastical sites have served as a key destination for pilgrims in the Holy Land. The town was the terminus of a pilgrimage route that began in Jerusalem before continuing north through Hebron. Approaching Bethlehem, the pilgrims would access the town via the Damascus Gate, one of the oldest entrances to the historic core of the town. Bethlehem was evidently enclosed by a high wall from Canaanite times, though it was demolished by the Mamluks in 1489.[109] The Damascus Gate managed to survive this incident, and remains in an excellent state of preservation.

---

[106] These bells were introduced to Bethlehem between 1227 and 1244, but under Turkish rule such bells were not allowed to be rung, and the bell towers were demolished. See Prag, 2000

[107] Prag, 2000

[108] Mertens, A., and Bannurah, Z. (1981) *Chronological Walk Through Bethlehem*. Jerusalem: Notre Dame of Jerusalem Center.

[109] Prag, 2000

Berthold Werner's picture of the Damascus Gate

Within Bethlehem, the pilgrims would travel along the historic Star Street, then along Paul VI Street to Manger Square and the Church of the Nativity.[110] This pilgrimage route is believed to follow the same path that Joseph and Mary followed on their journey from Nazareth to Bethlehem.

Star Street is a fascinating part of Bethlehem's heritage, as it features some of the best preserved Roman-Byzantine buildings in the city. Furthermore, it was historically the place of residence for the town's Tarajmeh

---

[110] Mertens and Bannurah, 1981

Clan, also known as "the Translators", and the Herezat Clan. These two families were two of the most famous manufacturers of crucifixes and models of the Nativity for pilgrims, as well as a variety of other objects made of mother of pearl and local olive wood. They have operated from Bethlehem for centuries.[111]

Pilgrims would also pass by the Milk Grotto, a subterranean shrine located south of the Church of the Nativity. The shrine was active since at least the 4th century, with a church constructed over the cave in 385.[112] A second church was erected in 1872 by the Franciscan community, though a modern chapel replaced this in 2007. Its name comes from the chalky white stone from which the cave was hollowed out, but legends also say that when Joseph and Mary were fleeing from Bethlehem before Herod's massacre of the innocents, a drop of milk fell from Mary's breast as she nursed the baby Jesus.[113] That drop made the stone in the area turn white. It is for this reason that the caves became a shrine to Our Lady of the Milk, and became a sacred place for both Christian and Muslim pilgrims. Many visitors were mothers of newly born children or women trying to conceive[114].

One of the more unusual customs carried out in the caves

[111] Mertens and Bannurah, 1981
[112] Gonen, 2000
[113] Gonen, 2000
[114] Gonen, 2000

was the mixing together of the soft chalk stone with their food before consuming it.[115] From the 7th century onwards pieces of the cave walls were removed and sent to churches across the Holy Land and Europe.

The Pilgrimage Route also passed by the Mosque of Omar, the only Muslim place of worship within the boundaries of the Old Town in Bethlehem. Built in 1860, the mosque was dedicated to Omar Ibn Al Khattab, caliph of the Umayyads and one of Mohammad's companions.[116] The land on which it was built was donated to the mosque by the Greek Orthodox Church. King David's Wells are also part of the route, being associated with the story of David being forced to find refuge from Saul's armies in the Cave of Adullam.[117]

Before entering the Church of the Nativity complex the pilgrims would have passed a large cistern cut into the limestone rock of the landscape. It was approximately 25 feet deep and filled with rainwater that passed through a carefully designed filtration system.[118] The cistern was lined with mortar, making it waterproof. It was also beautifully decorated; on the eastern wall was a carved cross pointing in the direction of the Church of the Nativity. This may also have been used for baptisms.

---

[115] Gonen, 2000
[116] Mertens and Bannurah, 1981
[117] Hyman, R. T. (2006) "Multiple Functions Of Wells In The Tanakh." *Jewish Bible Quarterly, 34*(3).
[118] Mertens and Bannurah, 1981

Pilgrims could then enter the forecourt of the Church of the Nativity, the religious heart of the town. This was the original atrium of the Constantinian church. Access was from the west; to the east was the church itself, to the south was the Armenian Convent, and to the north was a tall wall behind which is the Greek Orthodox cemetery. To the north was the Pilgrimage Residence, owned by the Greek Orthodox Church but operated by the Order of Saint Francis.[119] Each year, the Patriarchs of the three major Christian denominations represented at Bethlehem – the Western, Eastern, and Armenian churches – embark on the pilgrimage through the city.[120]

In 1887, the Irish Presbyterian missionary Josias Leslie Porter wrote extensively on the pilgrimage route, giving readers a unique perspective of Bethlehem before the developments of the 20th and 21st centuries encroached upon the Old Town: "Bethlehem is now before us, standing on a narrow ridge which project eastward from the central range of the hills of Judah, and break down in terraced slopes to deep glens on the north and south, and to a broad reach of table-land on the east. The terraces are covered in vineyards, and studded with olives; they sweep down the ridge regular as steps of stairs. On the eastern brow of the ridge, separated from the crowded village by an open esplanade, is the convent, like a large feudal

[119] Mertens and Bannurah, 1981
[120] Raheb, Strickert, Strickert, and Nalbandian, 1998

castle. It is a huge pile consisting of the Church of the Nativity and the three convents – Latin, Greek and Armenian abutting on its northeast and south sides."[121]

Porter

[121] Porter, J. L. (1886) *Jerusalem, Bethany and Bethlehem*. Ariel Publishing House

Bethlehem in the Modern Age

Bethlehem continued to have deep significance throughout the Ottoman era and in modern times, but it has also been subject to some of the most violent conflicts in the region. During the Ottoman period, beginning in the late 16th century, much work was conducted on the Church of the Nativity. Its marble floors were removed between 1596 and 1626 to be used in other building projects in the town,[122] and in 1670, the lead portions of the roof were stripped away to be used to manufacture ammunition, though it was restored by the Greek Orthodox community the following year.[123] They imported wood from Istanbul and hired carpenters from Chios and Mitylene to install a wooden iconostasis within the church.[124] The central doorway to the church was reduced again during this time.

In 1717, the iconic silver star was embedded on a white marble floor in the Cave of the Nativity upon the spot where Jesus was said to have been born.[125] This was inscribed with the text "Here Jesus Christ was born of the Virgin Mary."[126] In 1847 this star was stolen – an event that is said to have been a contributing factor in the beginning of the Crimean War (1854–1856).[127] In 1853 a

---

[122] Freeman-Grenville, 1993
[123] Cust, L. G. A., and Schiller, E. (1980). *Status quo in the holy places*. Jerusalem: Ari'el.
[124] Pringle, 1993
[125] Freeman-Grenville, 1993
[126] Freeman-Grenville, 1993

replacement star was offered by the Ottoman Sultan to replace that which was stolen. An earthquake in 1834 caused some damaged to the Church of the Nativity, though repairs started immediately and continued in 1842.[128] A fire broke out in 1869 that caused severe damage to the crypt, destroying most of its furnishings and damaging the ancient mosaics within.[129] Buttresses were erected against the church walls to try and mitigate some of the risk of collapse.

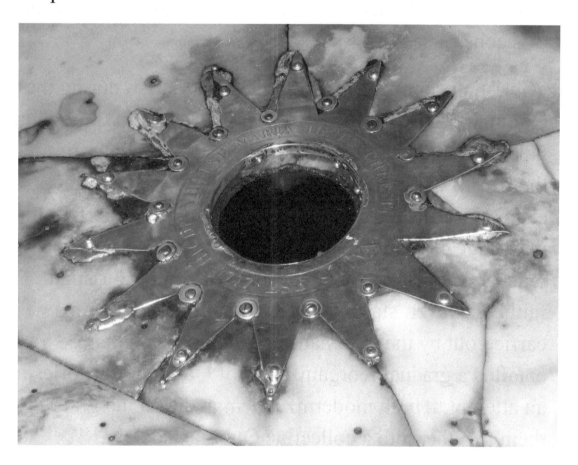

The star marking the spot where Christians believe

[127] Hamilton, 1968
[128] Freeman-Grenville, 1993
[129] Hunt, 1991

Jesus was born

Building works were carried out elsewhere in and around Bethlehem during the Ottoman period. In around 1875, the bell tower was erected on the former site of the Greek Orthodox Monastery. In 1938, the "Al Saraya", an Ottoman Governmental building that was constructed in 1873 near the Greek Orthodox cemetery, was burned down during the Palestinian uprising against the British Mandate.[130] The British Mandate Governmental building was constructed in its place.

Christian communities continued to flourish during the Ottoman occupation of Bethlehem, as they did throughout Palestine, and many missions from different countries in the world were established throughout the Holy Land, even after the Crusades. They provided local communities with education and medical services, and in doing so managed to bring many new converts to the Christian faith. However, starting in 1838 a number of reforms were carried out by the Ottomans called the "Tanzimat". This entailed a gradual reorganization of Ottoman territories in an attempt to both modernize them and also integrate them together into a collective Ottoman society.[131]

The modernization projects began in 1895 in Bethlehem,

---

[130] Mertens and Bannurah, 1981

[131] Abu-Manneh, B. (1990) "Jerusalem in the Tanzimat period: the new Ottoman administration and the notables." *Die Welt des Islams*, 1(4), 1 - 44.

resulting in the construction of Bethlehem's first school. One of the many policies followed was the opening up of Ottoman borders to foreigners. The number of pilgrims traveling to Bethlehem and other sites in the Holy Land increased dramatically. They traveled along an infrastructure much improved by the Ottomans and later by the British Mandate. It was from this point onward that the town began to grow outside of its original, enclosed historic center, with the old city walls of the Justinian period having been destroyed in 1489 under the orders of the Ottoman sultan Selim I.[132]

Throughout the 19th century, Palestine and the rest of the Holy Land was the focal point of Turkish, Russian, British, Austrian, French, and German attention. Napoleon assumed control of the town as late as 1852, a claim that brought him into conflict with Russia, which supported the Eastern Orthodox communities of Bethlehem.[133] This tension was settled with the Treaty of Berlin in 1878, an agreement that continues to influence how Bethlehem is governed to the present day.[134]

Military incidents continued in the new millennium. The Allied Powers reconvened in 1922 after the military defeat of the Ottoman Empire during World War I to

---

[132] Mertens and Bannurah, 1981

[133] Shulim, J. J. (1945) "Napoleon I as the Jewish Messiah: Some Contemporary Conceptions in Virginia." *Jewish Social Studies*, 275 - 280

[134] Raheb, Strickert, Strickert, and Nalbandian, 1998

discuss the mandates of the former Turkish territories. Their decisions created a new map for the Near East. It was decided that the Mandate for Palestine would serve as an internationally binding treaty different from those for Syria and Iraq.[135] Whilst the mandates for the latter focused on the Arab people living in those territories, the Mandate for Palestine did not just focus on the people within Palestine; Great Britain was given responsibility to follow through on the promises made in the articles of the mandate, which recognized the historical connection of the Jewish people worldwide to the land and their right to reconstitute a home in Palestine. Until the articles of this Mandate could be implemented throughout the territory, Great Britain was in charge of the administration in the former Ottoman lands.[136]

Between 1860 and 1948, Bethlehem enjoyed a period of relative peace and prosperity, and the British Mandate oversaw a great deal of urban development in the town. They employed more than 500 stonecutters and craftsmen to construct mansions, governmental buildings, and public services around Bethlehem.[137] Education and commerce improved, and trade agreements were made between Bethlehem and countries in East Asia, America, and Europe.[138]

---

[135] Segev, T. (2000) *One Palestine, complete: Jews and Arabs under the British mandate*. Macmillan.
[136] Segev, 2000
[137] Mertens and Bannurah, 1981
[138] Palestine Ministry of Tourism and Antiquities, 2011

However, they also caused some damage to Bethlehem's ecclesiastical heritage. In 1918, the Military Governor of Jerusalem, Sir Ronald Storrs, ordered that the chancel screen in the Church of the Nativity be destroyed.[139] Furthermore, there was a greater degree of social stratification as families became more wealthy, which meant that new and larger houses were sought in the most desirable – also frequently the older – parts of the town. Many historic structures were demolished as a result.

[139] Cobb, E. (2014) "Politics of Place in the Middle East and World Heritage Status for Jerusalem." In Mohammad, G. (Ed) *Sacred precincts: the religious architecture of non-muslim communities across the islamic world*. Brill. 123 - 140

Storrs

Bethlehem has been surveyed and recorded by a number of academics and non-academics from the time of the Old Testament onwards. The earliest of travelers passed through the town and made a brief mention of it during their journeys to and from Jerusalem. The town was visited by the Franciscan priest and antiquarian Bernardino Amico of Gallipoli in approximately 1596, and he subsequently produced some particularly fine illustrations of the Church of the Nativity.[140] From the

17th century onwards, more and more documentary accounts – including illustrations and photographs – began to be made of Bethlehem. In 1621, the English poet George Sandys – later a member of the council of the newly-formed state of Virginia – traveled throughout the Holy Lands in the 1610s and produced an excellent map and description of the pilgrimage route between Jerusalem and Bethlehem.[141]

A portrait of Sandys

The Church of the Nativity has contained a vast selection of furnishings and artifacts during its long history, many

[140] Palestine Ministry of Tourism and Antiquities, 2011
[141] Sandys, G. (1973) *A Relation of a Journey Begun An: Dom: 1610: Containing a Description of the Turkish Empire, of Egypt, of the Holy Land, of the Remote Parts of Italy, and Islands Adioyning.* Andrew Crooke.

of which were removed to museums and churches around the world, or buried and later found by archaeologists in the modern period. For example, in 1906, two sets of artifacts were discovered in Bethlehem: a collection of 13 copper bells from the 12th century that was part of the carillon that had once existed in the church bell tower, and a "water organ" consisting of 250 individual parts.[142] Found during the same season were two brass bowls dating from approximately 1140, each of which inscribed with scenes from the life of Saint Thomas, one of the Twelve Apostles.[143] There are still many fine icons, wood carvings, and statues within the present-day building, some of which date as far back as the 15th century. For this reason, the Church of the Nativity has been described as a veritable museum of Christian and Palestinian art.

Aside from the central church, most of Bethlehem has never been systematically excavated by archaeologists, and it is very likely that much evidence of life in the town during the centuries before and after Jesus's time remains to be discovered.

Between 1933 and 1935, limited excavations were conducted at the Church of the Nativity by the British Mandate in preparation for a structural survey of the building.[144] In 1935, parts of the external forecourt and the

---

[142] Prag, 2000
[143] Prag, 2000
[144] Prag, 2000

church interior were retiled, and in the process parts of the ancient Constantinian mosaic floor were uncovered.[145]

During the 1990s a comprehensive site assessment of the gardens to the east of the Church of the Nativity was conducted by the Palestine Exploration Fund.[146] Recent excavations have taken place to the northwest of Manger Square, undertaken by the Bethlehem Peace Center. During two seasons in 1999 and 2009, the remains of 5th and 6th century ruins were discovered in the location of the present-day Bethlehem Peace Center (the former British Mandate Governmental building and later Israeli police headquarters). They discovered additional mosaic floors, as well as the remains of a basilican chapel or monastery.[147]

As the birthplace of one of the world's major religions, Bethlehem continues to be a focus of the Jewish faith millennia after its origins, and alongside Jerusalem, Bethlehem is one of the most important sites in the Christian world. It also has an important role in the Islamic faith, in the role that the figure of Jesus played as the Muslim prophet Issa.

To this day, the question of whether Jesus Christ was born in the cave beneath the Church of the Nativity is a

---

[145] Kitzinger, 1970
[146] Prag, 2000
[147] Palestine Ministry of Tourism and Antiquities, 2011

matter of fierce debate, as it was only from approximately 329 that this narrative was introduced. However, it cannot be stressed enough how important that belief has been for diverse religious communities over the past 17 centuries. The complex of buildings that has grown in the old town of Bethlehem is unique, including the oldest church in the world that has been in continuous use since its construction, and other important buildings represent the gradual fragmentation and complexity of the Christian faith in later history. Greek Orthodox, Franciscan and Armenian congregations have all found a way to coexist within this sacred site, the importance of which crosses denominational boundaries.

Today, the city's inhabitants largely depend on tourists for their livelihood. Although Bethlehem's population is only 25,000, each year the site receives more than two million visitors.[148] It also serves as the main trade center for surrounding farming villages and pastoral nomads who still inhabit the area. The Greek Orthodox Church, Armenian Orthodox Church, and Franciscan Order continue to serve as the primary stakeholders and custodians of Bethlehem's ecclesiastical landscape, and they are responsible for the upkeep and use of the Church of Nativity and surrounding structures.

The outbreak and aftermath of the 1948 war between the

---

[148] Palestine Ministry of Tourism and Antiquities, 2011

Arabs and Israel following the contentious United Nations Partition Plan for Palestine in 1947 had a long-lasting effect on Bethlehem. A great number of refugees fled to Bethlehem, tripling its population from 9,000 to more than 35,000 almost overnight.[149] Since then, there have been periods of emigration from the town, especially following the Palestinian intifadas that began in 1987 and 2000. Since 1995, Bethlehem has officially been part of the Palestinian Authority, though Israel retains military control of the main access points to and from the region. During the Second Intifada, in an effort to stop suicide bombers emanating from the West Bank, Israel constructed a security fence, part of which runs along the northern side of the town, only feet away from the residential housing of the population, of which a majority is Muslim. The rest of the population is made up of Bedouin Arabs; Latin, Syrian, Melchite, Armenian and Maronite Catholics; Greek, Syrian and Armenian Orthodox communities; and a variety of Protestant denominations.[150]

The Church of the Nativity has a long narrative of alternating periods of ruin and repair, but these have been exacerbated in the modern period. The structure continues to the present day to suffer the effects of its long age, and for this reason it is commonly described as one of the

---

[149] Mertens and Bannurah, 1981
[150] Palestine Ministry of Tourism and Antiquities, 2011

most endangered heritage buildings in the world.[151] According to the World Monuments Fund, "The present state of the church is worrying. Many roof timbers are rotting, and have not been replaced since the 19th century. The rainwater that seeps into the building not only accelerates the rotting of the wood and damages the structural integrity of the building, but also damages the 12th-century wall mosaics and paintings. The influx of water also means that there is an ever-present chance of an electrical fire. If another earthquake were to occur on the scale of the one of 1834, the result would most likely be catastrophic. ... It is hoped that the listing will encourage its preservation, including getting the three custodians of the church – the Greek Orthodox Church, the Armenian Orthodox Church, and the Franciscan order – to work together, which has not happened for hundreds of years. The Israeli government and the Palestinian Authority would also have to work together to protect it."

The church's roof has been a focal point for the conservation projects that the building is subject to, having not been replaced since 1842. The rainwater that has seeped in over the centuries has caused irreparable damage to the mosaics and paintings inside the basilica. Furthermore, there have been frequent fires within the old buildings, and even occasional earthquakes have caused

---

[151] World Monuments Fund (2008) *2008 World Monuments Watch List Of 100 Most Endangered Sites.* World Monuments Fund.

damage the ecclesiastical complex. Between April and May 2001, the Church of the Nativity was the scene of fighting between Palestinians and Israeli military forces, which caused further damage to the structure.[152]

The rest of the heritage landscape at Bethlehem has also suffered in the modern period. Urban developments in 1956 drastically transformed that layout of Bethlehem, mainly according to the requirements of tourists, with new shops and hotels replacing many of the historic structures. Amongst the changes made were the relocation of the centuries-old marketplace near the Mosque of Omar and the demolition of the residential neighborhood north of the mosque.[153] The use of inappropriate or inauthentic building methods and materials for the reconstruction projects has generally worsened these deteriorating conditions as well. Most of all, the steadily increasing number of visitors arriving at Bethlehem each day – especially in the last few decades – has hastened the general worsening of the historic buildings and art.

Online Resources

Other books about ancient history by Charles River Editors

Other books about Christianity by Charles River Editors

---

[152] Palestine Ministry of Tourism and Antiquities, 2011
[153] Palestine Ministry of Tourism and Antiquities, 2011

Other books about Bethlehem on Amazon

Bibliography

Amara, Muhammad (1999). Politics and sociolinguistic reflexes: Palestinian border villages (Illustrated ed.). John Benjamins Publishing Company. ISBN 978-90-272-4128-3.

Brynen, Rex (2000). A very political economy: peacebuilding and foreign aid in the West Bank and Gaza (Illustrated ed.). US Institute of Peace Press. ISBN 978-1-929223-04-6.

Crossan, John Dominic; Watts, Richard G. "Who Is Jesus?: Answers to Your Questions About the Historical Jesus". Westminster John Knox Press.

Dunn, James D. G. (2003). Jesus Remembered: Christianity in the Making. Wm. B. Eerdmans Publishing. ISBN 978-0-8028-3931-2. Archived from the original on 2013-11-04. Retrieved 17 July 2011.

Freed, Edwin D. (2004). "Stories of Jesus' Birth". Continuum International.

Mills, Watson E.; Bullard, Roger Aubrey (1990). "Mercer Dictionary of the Bible". 5. Mercer University Press.

Petersen, Andrew (2005). The Towns of Palestine Under

Muslim Rule. British Archaeological Reports. ISBN 978-1-84171-821-7. Archived from the original on 2012-11-11.

Read, Peirs Paul (2000). The Templars. Macmillan. ISBN 978-0-312-26658-5.

Sanders, E. P. (1993). "The Historical Figure of Jesus".

Sawsan & Qustandi Shomali. Bethlehem 2000. A Guide to Bethlehem and it Surroundings.Waldbrol, Flamm Druck Wagener GMBH, 1997.

Singer, Amy (1994). Palestinian Peasants and Ottoman Officials: Rural Administration Around Sixteenth-Century Jerusalem. Cambridge University Press. ISBN 978-0-521-47679-9.

Strange, le, Guy (1890). Palestine Under the Moslems: A Description of Syria and the Holy Land from A.D. 650 to 1500. Committee of the Palestine Exploration Fund. Retrieved 2016-03-17.

Taylor, Joan E. (1993). "Christians and the Holy Places". Oxford University Press.

Thomson, Revered W.M. (1860). The Land and the Book.

Vermes, Geza (2006). "The Nativity: History and Legend". Penguin Press

Free Books by Charles River Editors

We have brand new titles available for free most days of the week. To see which of our titles are currently free, click on this link.

Discounted Books by Charles River Editors

We have titles at a discount price of just 99 cents everyday. To see which of our titles are currently 99 cents, click on this link.

Made in United States
Troutdale, OR
03/14/2024

18447851R00053